THE MIRACLE OF THE LOAVES AND FISHES

Bible Bedtime Story

BLUME POTTER

INTRODUCTION

In a world filled with endless distractions, finding a story that not only entertains but also instills timeless values can be a challenge. The Miracle of the Loaves and Fishes is more than just a collection of bedtime stories; it's a gentle way to introduce your child or grandchild to the incredible power of faith, compassion, and the joy of sharing.

This book retells one of the most beloved Bible stories in a way that is both captivating and easy to understand for young minds. Each chapter is a standalone tale that brings to life the miracle of Jesus feeding thousands with just a small boy's humble lunch. Through simple, yet engaging prose, your child will learn about the importance of kindness, the power of generosity, and the boundless love of God.

Perfect for bedtime, these stories will not only lull your little one to sleep with a sense of peace and security but will also plant seeds of faith and compassion in their hearts. As you read these stories together, you'll find that this book is more than just a storybook—it's a treasured opportunity to pass on values that will last a lifetime.

Make The Miracle of the Loaves and Fishes a part of your child or grandchild's bedtime routine, and watch as their love for these timeless lessons grows night after night.

CHAPTER ONE:
A DAY WITH JESUS

The sun was just beginning to rise, painting the sky with soft pinks and golds, as a large crowd began to gather. They had heard the stories—how Jesus healed the sick, made the blind see, and even raised the dead. People from all around came to see Him, to hear His words, and to feel His love.

Jesus led them to a grassy hillside, a peaceful place where everyone could sit and listen. As He spoke, the people were amazed. His words were like a gentle breeze, bringing comfort and hope. He spoke about God's love, telling them that each person was special and cared for, no matter who they were.

The day went on, and the crowd grew larger. Some brought their sick loved ones, hoping for a miracle. Jesus, with a kind smile and gentle touch, healed each one. The blind could see, the lame could walk, and the sick were made well. It was a day filled with joy and wonder.

But as the sun began to sink lower in the sky, the disciples started to worry. They whispered among themselves, looking out at the thousands of people who had gathered. "It's getting late," one of them said. "These people have been here all day, and they have nothing to eat."

Jesus looked at the crowd with compassion. He knew they were hungry, not just for food, but for something more— hope, love, and the truth of God's goodness. As He continued to teach, the disciples wondered how they could possibly feed so many with what little they had.

The day with Jesus had been extraordinary, but as evening approached, the disciples faced a new challenge. How would they provide for the crowd that had gathered, trusting in the man who spoke of miracles?

Little did they know, another miracle was just about to unfold.

CHAPTER TWO:
A SMALL BOY'S LUNCH

As the sun dipped closer to the horizon, the disciples grew more anxious. The crowd was vast—thousands of men, women, and children scattered across the hillside, all waiting expectantly. The disciples huddled together, their faces filled with concern.

"Master," one of them said, "it's getting late, and these people are hungry. We should send them away so they can find food in the nearby villages."

But Jesus shook His head gently. "No," He replied. "You give them something to eat."

The disciples looked at each other, puzzled. How could they possibly feed so many with nothing? They searched among the crowd, hoping to find some food, but all they found was a small boy with a simple lunch—five small loaves of bread and two fish.

The boy looked up at the disciples with wide eyes as they explained the situation. Without hesitation, he held out his lunch. "Here, take this," he said. "I want to help."

The disciples took the boy's lunch and brought it to Jesus. "This is all we have," they said, holding up the small basket. "But how can this little bit feed so many?"

Jesus smiled at the boy, a twinkle in His eye. He knew that the boy's simple act of kindness and faith was more than enough. Taking the small basket in His hands, Jesus turned to the disciples and said, "Have the people sit down."

The disciples did as they were told, still unsure of what would happen next. They knew that what they had wasn't nearly enough to feed such a large crowd, but they trusted Jesus. The small boy, now standing close to Jesus, watched with hopeful eyes, wondering what He would do with his tiny offering.

The stage was set for something miraculous, something that would show everyone present that with Jesus, even the smallest offering could be more than enough.

CHAPTER THREE:
JESUS BLESSES THE FOOD

The crowd sat down on the soft grass, murmuring among themselves, curious about what Jesus would do next. The disciples stood nearby, holding the small boy's lunch—just five loaves of bread and two fish. It seemed impossible that such a small meal could feed so many people.

But Jesus was calm and confident. He took the loaves and fish in His hands and looked up to heaven. With a gentle voice, He gave thanks to God for the food, blessing it with a prayer of gratitude. The disciples watched closely, their hearts filled with a mix of wonder and uncertainty.

After giving thanks, Jesus began to break the bread and fish into pieces. He handed the pieces to the disciples and said, "Give these to the people."

The disciples obeyed, taking the bread and fish and starting to distribute it to the crowd. As they did, something amazing happened—the bread and fish didn't run out. No matter how many pieces they handed out, there was always more. Basket after basket was filled and passed around, and the food kept multiplying.

The people ate and ate, their hunger satisfied by the meal that had started as just a small boy's lunch. The disciples moved among the crowd, sharing the food with everyone, marveling at the miracle unfolding before their eyes.

By the time everyone had eaten their fill, more than 5,000 people had been fed, and there was still food left over. The small boy who had given his lunch stood in awe, realizing that his simple gift had been turned into something extraordinary by Jesus.

The crowd was amazed and filled with joy. They knew they had witnessed something special, something that showed the power of Jesus' love and the greatness of God's provision.

As the evening sky deepened into shades of purple and orange, the people knew that this day was one they would never forget—a day when a small offering became a miracle in the hands of Jesus.

CHAPTER FOUR:
EVERYONE IS SATISFIED

The disciples moved through the crowd, handing out the bread and fish that Jesus had blessed. At first, they were cautious, unsure if there would be enough for everyone. But as they continued to pass out the food, they realized that no matter how much they gave, there was always more.

The people ate with gratitude, enjoying the unexpected feast. They couldn't believe their eyes—what had started as a small boy's lunch had become a meal for thousands. Mothers fed their children, friends shared with one another, and the entire hillside buzzed with happiness and amazement.

The disciples, too, were in awe. They had never seen anything like this before. As they distributed the food, their baskets seemed to magically refill, overflowing with bread and fish. It was as if the food would never run out.

Finally, after everyone had eaten their fill, the crowd leaned back, content and satisfied. Not a single person was left hungry. The disciples, still in disbelief at what had happened, returned to Jesus.

Jesus looked at them with a gentle smile and said, "Gather the leftovers, so nothing is wasted."

The disciples did as He asked. They went back through the crowd, collecting what remained. To their astonishment, they filled twelve large baskets with leftover bread and fish. The small meal that had seemed barely enough for one person had not only fed thousands but had also provided more than they could have imagined.

The people marveled at the sight. They knew they had witnessed a miracle—something that showed them the limitless love and provision of Jesus. As they prepared to leave, they couldn't stop talking about the incredible day they had just experienced.

The disciples, carrying the baskets of leftovers, were filled with wonder and gratitude. They knew that with Jesus, nothing was impossible, and that even the smallest offering, given in faith, could be turned into something miraculous.

CHAPTER FIVE:
THE MIRACLE OF SHARING

As the crowd began to disperse, whispers of excitement and wonder spread among them. They knew they had witnessed something truly extraordinary—a miracle that would be remembered for generations. The small boy who had given his lunch stood quietly, his heart swelling with joy. He had learned that even the smallest gift, when given with love and kindness, could make a big difference.

Jesus gathered the people around Him one last time before they left. His voice was warm and gentle as He spoke, "Today, you have seen the power of God's love. With just five loaves and two fish, thousands of you were fed. This is a reminder that God's love is abundant, and when we share what we have, no matter how small, it can be multiplied to bless many."

The people listened intently, their hearts touched by His words. They realized that the miracle they had witnessed was not just about food, but about the power of sharing and compassion. Jesus had taken a small boy's simple lunch and turned it into a feast for thousands, showing them that even the smallest act of kindness could have a huge impact.

The little boy smiled, feeling proud and grateful. He knew that his small act of sharing had been part of something much bigger than himself. The crowd left the hillside that evening, their hearts full of joy and their minds filled with the lessons they had learned.

As the last of the people walked away, the disciples gathered around Jesus, their baskets still full of the leftovers. They, too, were amazed by what they had seen and heard. Jesus looked at them with a knowing smile and said, "Remember this day, and always be willing to share what you have. God's love is more than enough for everyone."

The miracle of the loaves and fishes had not only filled the people's stomachs but also their hearts. It was a day that taught them all about the importance of sharing, the power of kindness, and the limitless love of God. And as they returned to their homes, they carried with them the memory of that miraculous day, eager to share what they had learned with others.